Richard Frederick Clarke

University Education in Ireland

A retrospect and a prospect

Richard Frederick Clarke

University Education in Ireland
A retrospect and a prospect

ISBN/EAN: 9783337035921

Printed in Europe, USA, Canada, Australia, Japan

Cover: Foto ©Paul-Georg Meister /pixelio.de

More available books at **www.hansebooks.com**

UNIVERSITY EDUCATION IN IRELAND:

A RETROSPECT AND A PROSPECT.

BY

RICHARD F. CLARKE, S.J.,

Formerly Fellow and Tutor of St. John's College, Oxford.

LONDON
LONGMANS, GREEN, AND CO.
AND NEW YORK: 15 EAST 16th STREET.

1890.

PREFACE.

IN the following pages, which are in substance a Reprint from *The Month*, I have endeavoured to sketch, under the guidance of those who have been longer in the country, and have a better knowledge of it than myself, the outlines of a plan for the settlement of the University Education Question in Ireland. I should scarcely have ventured to publish them, had not my experience at Oxford and elsewhere convinced me that a solution of it is perfectly possible at the present time.

The plan I am putting forward has for its object to reconcile, as far as may be, the various conflicting interests concerned.

1. It aims at the establishment of a National University, with subordinate Colleges, which shall gather into itself, and bring to perfection, so far as may be, all the talent and mental activity, which now to a great extent lies undeveloped.

2. It is a scheme of education in accordance with the true principles of an enlightened Conservatism, preserving to already existing institutions all that they possess, and rendering efficient what was before hampered by restrictive enactments, or the absence of external aid.

3. It deserves the support of all true Liberals, as it legislates for the Irish nation in accordance with what they themselves desire, and brings into healthy competition the various religious denominations of the country in the examination arena of a common University.

4. It guards the interest of the Episcopalian Protestants of Ireland, as it leaves Trinity College, with its revenues, buildings, estates, &c., entirely untouched.

5. It does justice to the talent and energy of the Presbyterian body, as it puts the Queen's College, Belfast, in their hands, and at the same time augments its present revenues in recognition of the excellent service that it has rendered to education in Ireland.

6. It provides for the Catholics of Ireland what they have for long years been claiming, in one form or other, for the sacred cause of Catholic education,

and puts them in the position due to them in a country, to which none can deny the title of "Catholic Ireland."

In the course of these pages I hope that the reader will find that my proposal is one that will meet the general wishes of the community. As many of those into whose hands this pamphlet may fall, may not have time to read it carefully, I will briefly state here the guiding features of my plan.

What I propose is as follows:

1. The establishment, side by side with Trinity, under a common University of two endowed University Colleges, one Catholic, in Dublin, the other Presbyterian, in Belfast or elsewhere.

2. The endowment of the Catholic College in a degree which shall bear some sort of proportion to the present endowment of non-Catholic Colleges. The calculation of the endowment that may be claimed is based on the proportion of boys from Catholic and Protestant schools respectively, who pass through the two higher grades of intermediate education. This proportion is, on an average of the last three years, fourteen Catholics to eleven Protestants, and I thence infer that the endowment of Catholic University

Colleges should be to the endowment of Protestant University Colleges, as fourteen to eleven.[1]

3. The increase of the annual grant to Queen's College, Belfast, in proportion to its numbers, and the transference of the College into the hands of the Presbyterian and non-Episcopalian portion of the Protestants of Ireland.

4. The insertion of a Conscience Clause, to be enforced in all Colleges which shall be gathered under the National University, and the refusal of any grant of public money for the endowment of any Theological Professorship whatever, whether Catholic or Protestant.

These are the main features of the scheme. I omit all details, [as *e.g.*, the question of affiliated colleges, and of the means by which the Queen's Colleges of Cork and Galway may be adapted to the wants of the local population], since I do not wish to obscure the main question.

I have to thank His Grace the Archbishop of Dublin for his kindness in reading through my proof

---

[1] If we make our calculation from the existing revenues devoted to non-Catholic purposes, this would give to Catholics an annual grant of £80,000. This is a very large sum. But a re-adjustment of the revenues of Cork and Galway in favour of the population amid which they are placed would reduce this sum by nearly one half.

sheets, and making many valuable corrections. It is to him that the publication of this pamphlet is really due, though the plan that I am putting forward is entirely my own. It was suggested by one of the masterly addresses delivered by him on the Education question, and is little more than an indication of what seems to me the best way of attaining the "equality," which was the text of one of his discourses.

I have also to thank the Very Rev. Dr. Molloy for many valuable hints, and the Rev. Father Delany, S.J., for his kind assistance in drawing up the statistics on which my calculations are based.

University College, Dublin,
March 19, 1890.

UNIVERSITY EDUCATION IN IRELAND.

I.

ONE of the characteristics of the present condition of Ireland that appears most remarkable to one who comes from another land to dwell among her people is the almost unlimited amount of her undeveloped resources. Undeveloped productiveness in her soil, undeveloped skill and activity in her sons, undeveloped industries, undeveloped material prosperity, undeveloped stores of possible wealth, undeveloped talent of the most varied kind,—all these lie around on every side in rich profusion. The causes why these manifold treasures are still treasures *in posse* rather than *in esse*, treasures hereafter to be enjoyed by her children, rather than already at disposal for their use, are matters into which we need not enter now. Some already belong, through God's mercy, to the past, though their consequences still linger. Others flourish with a vigour apparently the same as ever, though their strength is more seeming than real, and the violence of their advocates is partly due to the secret consciousness that their days are numbered.

These causes, whatever they may be, have acted, some directly, by crushing out or rendering impossible the exercise of the activity which strove in vain to develope itself, others indirectly, by cutting off the sources of life and the means of nourishment. The struggling energy, deprived of the means of support necessary to it, died what seemed to be a natural death, though its premature decease was really due to a process of slow starvation. Even if its vigour enabled it to survive the secret efforts to destroy it, yet it had little or no chance of growing up to a strong and vigorous manhood. Any one who may desire to study in detail the method of operation of these destructive influences will find it written on almost every page of the past history of Ireland. It is not our task to reproduce those painful records, though we may indeed have to refer to them, once and again, in order to explain the present condition of that form of undeveloped activity which alone concerns us now.

The undeveloped activity of which we propose to treat in these pages is the undeveloped mental energy which we know by the name of "intelligence" or "talent." We employ the double term designedly, because "intelligence" is sometimes taken to mean the mere quickness of intellect which gives the power of rapid apprehension, rather than of retaining and reproducing the knowledge apprehended, to say nothing of the nobler gift that adds a creative element of its own. "Talent," on the other hand, is rather too wide a term for our present purpose, if it be separated from the kindred word, and would include other than purely intellectual activity. When, therefore, we say that there exists in Ireland a vast amount of undeveloped intelligence and talent, we desire to convey to our readers the conviction we entertain—and one which we imagine is beyond dispute—that there is to be found there a rich store of that intellectual power of acquiring, retaining, and turning knowledge to good account, which enables the nation that possesses it to rise high amid the nations of the earth in mental culture and true civilization.

The history of Ireland in early days gives us some idea of the place that she has a right to claim for the native talent of her children. There was a time when her schools were renowned throughout Christendom Before the Scandinavian invader had swept over the country with fire and sword, the Irish monasteries, by common consent, carried off the palm among the seats of learning that were scattered over Europe, and were held in such high esteem as to attract a large number of foreign ecclesiastics to study in their schools. It was Ireland that sent forth St. Virgilius, the anticipator of the Copernican system, to be Bishop of Salzburg, and to spread through all Germany the fame of his genius and of his sanctity. It was Ireland that gave birth to John Scotus Erigena, equally famous for varied erudition and for the daring boldness of his philosophical speculations. It was from Ireland that there went forth St. Columbanus and St. Gall, the former to evangelize England, Burgundy, and Northern Italy, the latter to give his name to one of the Swiss Cantons, and to a seat of learning still rich in Irish manuscripts and Irish literature. It was among the Irish divines, if we may trust to the authority of Moore's history of his own country, that Scholastic Philosophy had its first origin, and if his ideas of what Scholastic Philosophy really is are not very accurate, yet at least his testimony is valuable as evidence of the general belief in the initiative power of the Irish intellect in those early days.[1]

[1] "In the eighth century, indeed, the high reputation of the Irish scholarship had become established throughout Europe; and that mode of applying the learning and subtlety of the schools to the illustration of theology, which assumed at a later period a more systematic form under the name of the Scholastic Philosophy, is allowed to have originated among the eminent divines whom the monasteries of Ireland in the course of the century poured forth." (Moore's *History of Ireland*, i. 289.)

There was also another branch of learning in which Ireland won a name for itself in the seventh and eighth centuries. It is one we should have scarcely expected in a Western isle. The Irish were held in high esteem as Greek scholars. Eastern monks had brought with them a knowledge of their classic tongue, and some Irish students had returned with them to drink in the learning of the East. Hence arose a familiar acquaintance with Greek in many a monastery in Ireland. Sedulius, the well-known commentator, and Aileran, Abbot of Clonard, St. Virgil and Erigena, Augustine the monk, and Marianus Scotus, were all of them finished Greek scholars. Not a few, moreover, were acquainted with Hebrew, like Aileran above mentioned, who finds in the meaning of the names of all our Lord's ancestors a prophecy of Himself, and Sedulius,[1] who continually refers to the original Hebrew in his *Commentaries on Holy Scripture*.

We touch upon these details, not so much because of their historical interest, as because they have a very important bearing on the question before us. They prove that when the genius of Catholic Ireland was free to develope itself without let or hindrance, it took the lead in Europe, not merely in that kind of learning (if any such exists) that demands merely a receptive intelligence, but also in fields of research that require creative power, fearless speculation, and a readiness to enter on paths almost untrodden before. If (though we do not admit that it is the case) the country at the present day is slow to manifest the same characteristics that it displayed of yore, it is because its longing after

---

[1] Sedulius the Commentator is to be carefully distinguished from Sedulius the Christian poet, who was also an Irishman, and lived considerably earlier.

learning has so long been kept back by restrictive and prohibitive laws, and its power to initiate has been atrophied by measures which either forbade cultivation, except at the price of apostacy, or at least withheld from it that necessary support and maintenance without which a vigorous and healthy life is impossible to it. So we sometimes see a plant which comes, indeed, of healthy stock, but has been starved and almost destroyed by the cruel blasts of the east wind, and by some blight which robbed the soil in which it is planted of the fertilizing influences without which it is impossible for it to bear fruit. It still bears, indeed, clear marks of all that it has suffered. But restore to it the nourishment so cruelly denied it ; shield it from the cutting east, and let the sun's genial rays pour into it fresh life and strength ; remove from it whatever checked and stunted its capacity for development, and then you will soon see it reassume the force and energy of the parent stock, and clothe itself one by one with all the varied beauties of the past. Its former splendours seemed, indeed, to be diminished or even lost, but all the time remained latent in all their substantial vigour, ready to manifest themselves once again in their pristine comeliness, as soon as some kindlier influence shall bring them forth once more into the light of day.

The Danish invasion, and the unsettled condition of the country that continued for centuries afterwards, was fatal to the higher education of Ireland. The monasteries were never able to recover the prosperity of the seventh and eighth centuries. Intestine wars and private feuds seemed to divert the thoughts of men from higher things. Civil wars were the occasion of inviting English aid, and the whole country gradually fell under the sway of the invader. The disturbed condition of the whole of Ireland was ruinous to every kind of mental culture or higher education, and from Brian Boru until the Tudor dynasty became masters of England, the history of Ireland was little else than a continuous tale of struggles with foes without and foes within, of rebellion and counter-rebellion, of private quarrels between chief and chief, mingled with futile attempts to combine against the common foe. The wild lawlessness that accompanied the desperate struggles after freedom was no less fatal to religion and learning alike, than the rapacity and corruption, the selfish ambition and grasping tyranny that mark this disastrous period of Irish history.

If this period was disastrous, what shall we say of the period that succeeded it? Up to the time that Henry the Eighth threw off his allegiance to Rome, there had been no direct and positive hindrance to Catholic education in Ireland. The monasteries had declined, not through any hostile attitude of any of the various combatants who had striven for dominion, but simply because religious life and literary pursuits are always impossible in a country where violence prevails, and where there is no security for life and property. All through those troublous times the clergy, both secular and regular, and especially the Franciscan friars, did what they could in the cause of education, and their pious labours met with grateful acknowledgment from all, of whatever race or nation. It is true indeed that the English had burned the Irish abbeys and the Irish had retaliated on those of the Pale. But this was owing to no anti-religious feeling, but simply to the exigencies of war, and to the fact that the monks themselves too often forgot that they were servants of the Prince of Peace, in the eagerness of their political partisanship.

But when the Act of Supremacy was passed, and Henry sought to carry out in Ireland the policy that was so successful in his own country, there arose in Ireland a contest altogether different from any that had been seen before. The Irish people rose against the sacrilegious Reformers, sinking their mutual jealousies in presence of such a foe. With the exception of the appointment of a certain number of schismatical bishops, and the compliance of the officers of the English Crown with the commands of their imperious master, the reformed religion made no sort of way in Ireland in the reign of Henry or of Edward. It was not till Elizabeth ascended the throne that the struggle really began. We will draw a veil over the hideous and inhuman atrocities that disgraced the reign of terror which reached its climax under the bloody hand of Cromwell. We will merely glance as we pass on, at one or two attempts that were made even in the early days of Protestant domination in Ireland, to establish in the country some system of higher education for Catholics.

In 1564, on the strength of the tendency to lenient measures shown by Elizabeth in her early days, the first effort was made to found a Catholic University College. There is still extant a Bull of Pius the Fourth, in which he gives faculties to Richard Creagh, Archbishop of Armagh, and to David Wolfe, an Irish Jesuit, to employ for this purpose the funds arising from certain vacant benefices. To them was joined by the order of Father Lainez, who was then General of the Society, an English Jesuit named William Good, who had received his education at the University of Oxford.[1] But on their arrival

---

[1] "Nos igitur cupientes in civitatibus seu oppidis vel locis ejusdem Insulæ ad hoc commodioribus Universitates studiorum generalium ac Collegia erigi et institui, . . . Venerabili Fratri Nostro Richardo Crevoch,

in the country, they soon found that the scheme had no chance of success. If the Queen was inclined to a liberal policy, not so the Irish Executive, on account of whose opposition the project had to be speedily abandoned. Five years later, the Blessed Edmund Campion, having for conscience sake resigned his position and emoluments in the University of Oxford, came over to Ireland in the hope of being able to set on foot a University there. He was lodged in the house of his old friend and Oxford pupil, James Stanihurst, who was then Recorder of Dublin, and Speaker of the Irish House of Commons. Sir Philip Sidney was Lord Deputy at the time, and favoured the project of a University. Through his influence Campion, though suspected of being a Papist, was left unmolested to try and bring about his plan. But when the Lord Deputy quitted the country he had to give up all hopes of carrying it out. He remained, however, for six weeks longer in Dublin, and occupied his time in writing his *History of Ireland*, which was not so much a history as a pamphlet written with the object of showing that education was the great want of the country, if it was to make the social and intellectual progress necessary to unite it by the ties of a common civilization with the land from which he came.

moderno et pro tempore existenti Archiepiscopo Armacano totius Hiberniæ Primati, ac dilecto filio Davidi Wolfe, Presbytero Societatis Jesu in Hibernia existenti, et eorum cuilibet concedimus applicari et appropriari ex quibuscumque sæcularibus et Regularibus beneficiis ac locis Ecclesiasticis fructus et ædificia, ut, bonorum omnium largitore cooperante, hujusmodi miseriis feliciter obvietur, et tandem in dicta Hibernia viri eruditi et Doctores succedant, qui Ecclesiam Dei non opprimant, sed illam ex propriis bonis promoveant. Motu proprio (concedimus) Richardo ac Davidi præfatis (ut ab iis erigantur) Universitates ad instar Universitatum studiorum generalium Parisiensium et Lovaniensium, ac Collegia." (Hogan's *Ibernia Ignatiana*, pp. 14, 15.)

In 1630 another effort was made in behalf of the higher education of Catholics in Dublin, which at first showed good promise of success. A large collegiate building was erected in Back Lane, between Christ Church and the Cathedral of St. Patrick, and was opened as a College of higher studies under the management of the Jesuit Father, John Malone. But after two years of useful work, the nascent University was suppressed by the English Government, and the premises it had occupied were handed over to Trinity College.

The next hundred and fifty years witnessed a system of persecution, which has scarcely a parallel, even in pagan times. During the whole of this period, not only were Irish Catholics left without any sort of higher education, but education of every kind whatever was penal. Statute after statute was passed prohibiting and punishing any kind of mental training that Catholics could conscientiously accept. It was felony for a Catholic to act as teacher, and it was civil death for his pupils. Hence arose the now proverbial "hedge-school," at which the pupils watched by turn, lest they should be surprised at their forbidden studies by the Government spy, and the fees at which were sometimes paid in sods of turf, the pupils in their poverty having nothing else to offer. In their paternal care for the religious welfare for the poor Irish, the English Government forbade his education in other lands where he could be trained in his own faith. Any one going abroad for his education became *ipso facto* an outlaw. Sometimes indeed the smuggling craft that ran silks and brandy from France into the creeks of the southern coast had for their passengers priests or laymen who were eager after learning; but the number was necessarily small, and the great mass of the people had to choose between illiteracy and disloyalty to their faith. With all her passionate love of learning, with all her yearning desire after education, Catholic Ireland preferred the reproach of barbarism and utter ignorance, rather than imperil in the well-endowed Protestant schools and colleges which abounded in the country, the precious and inalienable heritage of her faith.

This state of things continued in all its persecuting vigour until the year 1783, when the most cruel of these penal laws were repealed. From that time those that were not actually abolished were allowed to fall into desuetude. But even primary education took many years to recover from two centuries of persecution; and higher education had altogether disappeared from Catholic Ireland. Intellectual cultivation in its higher forms is a plant of slow growth; it is the offspring of long tradition; it requires not only a bright and keen intelligence on the part of those who are to enjoy its riper fruits, not only an eager desire for knowledge, and a persevering and self-denying pursuit of it, but external facilities for its attainment. It also needs favourable environment, and that not for a year or for a decade, but for centuries. Even with the most able teaching and every encouragement, it makes at first but a slow advance unless there be hereditary culture in those who pursue it. Those who draw contrasts unfavourable to Ireland between the culture of her sons and those of the nation that rules her, would do well to remember that it was the double dose of the spirit of barbarous intolerance that crushed her efforts after learning and rendered the higher culture impossible to her. England, if she is to be worthy of the power that she wields, has not only to extend to her equal justice in matters of education in the present, but also to obliterate the sad memories of the cruel past, by a generosity that shall correspond in some degree to the fanatical bigotry which was formerly the keynote of her Irish policy.

It was in the year 1880, just two hundred and fifty years after the suppression of the College in Back Lane, that England took the first step towards a new attitude in the matter of the higher training, and offered to Irish Catholics an educational institution of which they could avail themselves without the violation of the claims of conscience. The Royal University, though not a University in the strict and proper sense of the term, inasmuch as it only examines and rewards those who belong to it, without undertaking as such any of the functions of a teaching body, was nevertheless an enormous boon to Catholic Education. If we are about to urge the claims of Ireland to further aid in the training of her children, it is not because we do not appreciate the importance of the step that has been already taken in the right direction. Our object will be to point out that the good work begun is but a first-fruits of what has to be done, if Catholics are to be treated with any approach to fair-dealing justice in comparison to their Protestant fellow-countrymen.

In order to establish our position, we must briefly survey the various endowed Universities and University Colleges already in existence. These are four in number: (1) The University of Dublin, with which Trinity College is for all practical purposes identical: (2) Queen's College, Belfast: (3) Queen's College, Cork: (4) Queen's College, Galway. The three last were united together under a corporation entitled the Queen's University, which conferred degrees till it was superseded by the Royal University in 1880.

We will begin with Trinity College. It was founded by Elizabeth in 1591, out of the sequestrated revenues of All Hallows Monastery, and had for its avowed object the education of the upper classes in Ireland in the Protestant religion, and more especially of training the ministers of the new religion in Protestant orthodoxy, in order that they might be so prepared to occupy the many vacant benefices and fight the battle of Anglicanism against the Faith that it was intended to replace. "The design of the English Queen (says Father Jouvancy, in his *History of the Society of Jesus*), was that the College she established should prove a bulwark of error, and at the same time a storehouse of armour and weapons for the Protestant clergy." He tells us that Catholics were invited to send their children thither, and were promised that they should have all the expenses of their education paid by the Government; an offer which was accepted by some few, who were men of lukewarm charity and straitened means. "But happily the children, wiser than their parents (we are quoting the words of the Catholic historian), having no fancy for wolves as their masters, forsook with one consent the school of error."[1]

James the First, anxious to remedy the deplorable ignorance of the Protestant ministers in Ireland, added very largely to the revenues of the College out of the confiscated estates of Irish recusants, and Trinity has

---

[1] "Hanc olim Academiam (Dublinensem) a Romanis Pontificibus institutam, deinde temporum injuria collapsam Elizabetha nuper instauraverat, eo consilio, ut esset in Hibernia propugnaculum erroris et simul armamentarium. Invitaverat parentes etiam Catholicos, ut eo liberos mitterent erudiendos gratis et alendos. Ea spes orthodoxos aliquot allexerat, quibus frigidior caritas atque res familiaris angustior; sed liberi parentibus sapientiores, magistros exosi lupos, scholam erroris unanimi consensu deseruerunt." (Jouvancy, *Hist. Soc. Jesu*, quoted in Hogan's *Ibernia Ignatiana*, pp. 32, 33.)

been from that day to this the home of cultivated Protestant orthodoxy in Ireland. As at the beginning, so throughout its whole existence it has done its best to draw young Catholics to study within its walls. Unlike the Universities of Oxford and Cambridge, it exacted no test from the student on his entrance within its walls ; but all its prizes, emoluments, and distinctions were withheld from all who did not conform to the religion that was dominant there and that formed the basis of its intellectual training. The Catholics who were educated there lost, with a few remarkable exceptions, the brightness and keenness of their faith. To no inconsiderable number Trinity was not only injurious, but absolutely fatal. Tempted by the brilliant worldly prospects which opened out before them if they shook themselves free of the disabilities of Popery, and with their faith already weakened by the atmosphere in which they lived, they ended in a shameful apostacy, or at least in giving up the practice of the religion which Trinity had taught them to despise.

But it is with the present, and not with the past that we are now more immediately concerned. Since the passing of Mr. Fawcett's Bill in 1873, the scholarships, fellowships, and other prizes offered to those educated at Trinity, have been subject to no religious restriction whatever. But as far as Catholics were concerned, it was a thankless boon that was thus conferred. The step was one taken in the direction of godless, as opposed to denominational education, and however strong the feeling of Catholics against any system of religion outside the Church, their feeling in respect of a system that ignores religion altogether, is far stronger. The very doubtful benefit conferred upon them, even if it did not carry with it the perils that it does, would have been one that the very principles of their faith taught them to regard with far less favour than the previous exclusiveness of the Protestant College. Trinity in fact is still practically closed to the Catholic youth of Ireland. It is true that a certain number are to be found there; and though we are of opinion that it is only by a miracle, or at all events by a very special Providence of Almighty God, that they can avoid losing the "keen edge" of their faith, yet we should be sorry to throw any unnecessary stone, and besides are sure from our own personal knowledge, that some at least there are who have, through God's good Providence, come out of Trinity unharmed. But the exception proves the rule, and the parent who sends his son to Trinity, does so in the teeth of many a warning from the Holy See, as well from local authorities, against the dangers to faith and morals that such an education carries with it.

The almost infinitesimal proportion of Catholic students at Trinity to the population is, however, the best proof of the practical rejection of the College by those who form the great bulk of the nation. The Catholics of the country outnumber the Protestants in the proportion of at least four to one, and would accordingly form, if there in due proportion, eighty per cent. of the students at Trinity. Yet the young Catholics there are only six per cent. of the whole number. In other words, Catholics are practically shut out from education there for conscience sake, and the undenominational, or rather the godless system prevailing there since 1873, so far from opening its doors to them, has rendered them more opposed than ever to the education given within its walls.

From Trinity we turn to the three Queen's Colleges

of Belfast, Cork, and Galway. These Colleges were established in the year 1849, mainly through the instrumentality of Sir Robert Peel, though Lord John Russell was Premier of the English Government at the time. They were originally united into one moral whole under the name of the Queen's University, and were an honest and praiseworthy attempt on the part of English statesmen to provide the Catholics of Ireland with a form of University education of which they could avail themselves without any violation of conscience. They were provided with magnificent buildings, splendid lecture-rooms and laboratories, libraries more than sufficient for all their needs, and every other material appliance requisite for their complete success. They were richly endowed, and the professorships were sufficiently lucrative to attract some of the best men from the English Universities and from Trinity College. They were also free from the religious restrictions that prevailed at Trinity, and that made it almost intolerable to any save those who belonged to the Established Religion. All their scholarships, prizes, professorships, nay, the very Presidency of its Colleges were opened freely to all denominations, and it was generally understood that in the parts of the country where the great mass of the population, and consequently by far the larger proportion of those seeking for the higher education, were Catholics, the office of President should be filled by a Catholic priest or layman. The scheme aimed throughout at a tender regard for the Catholic conscience, as well as at an impartial generosity.

It is true that they now are commonly spoken of by the name O'Connell gave them of the "godless Colleges," and are discountenanced, though not actually forbidden by the ecclesiastical authorities to Catholic students as places of education. But this was not at all the light in which they were regarded at their first institution. Doctor Murray was then Archbishop of Dublin. He was a prelate who had frequent and friendly communications with the officials of the Castle. The plan of the Queen's University was submitted to him and received his grateful recognition. Nor was he alone in regarding the new scheme as a welcome boon to Irish Catholics, and one that removed in great measure all cause of complaint in the matter of the higher education. Several members of the Irish Hierarchy shared his sentiments, though others looked upon the scheme as a well meant but none the less dangerous endeavour on the part of the English Liberals to introduce a system altogether at variance with Catholic principles.

The new University and its constituent Colleges were from the first the occasion of a somewhat bitter controversy among the lay, as well as the clerical, friends of Catholic education in Ireland. O'Connell denounced them from the very beginning. Thomas Davis, on the other hand, warmly espoused their cause. The matter was referred to the assembled Catholic Bishops, who decided in favour of the Bill on condition of certain resolutions passed by them and safeguarding the faith and morals of the Catholic students, being inserted, at least in substance, as amendments to the proposed measure. Without these amendments they declared it impossible to give their approbation to it. Their resolutions were embodied in a petition, which was entrusted to O'Connell for presentation to Parliament.[1]

---

[1] The memorial of the Bishops to the English Parliament was as follows:

"To His Excellency Lord Heytesbury, Lord-Lieutenant General and General Governor of Ireland.

"The Memorial of the Roman Catholic Archbishops and Bishops

The Government made several concessions, but refused those which the Bishops regarded as of vital importance. The appointment of Professors was to be entirely in the hands of the English Government, and all endowment was refused to the Principal of any College or Hall that was exclusively Catholic. O'Connell returned to Ireland and announced that the Government would

of Ireland humbly showeth—That Memorialists are disposed to co-operate, on fair and reasonable terms, with Her Majesty's Government and the Legislature, in establishing a system for the further extension of academical education in Ireland.

"That the circumstances of the present population of Ireland afford plain evidence that a large majority of the students belonging to the middle classes will be Roman Catholics; and Memorialists, as their spiritual pastors, consider it their indispensable duty to secure to the utmost of their power the most effectual means of protecting the faith and morals of the students in the new Colleges, which are to be erected for their better education.

"That a fair proportion of the professors, and other office-bearers in the new Colleges, should be members of the Roman Catholic Church, whose moral conduct shall have been properly certified by testimonials of character, signed by their respective prelates. And that all the office-bearers in those Colleges should be appointed by a board of trustees, of which the Roman Catholic prelates of the provinces in which any of those Colleges should be erected, shall be members.

"That the Roman Catholic pupils could not attend the lectures on history, logic, metaphysics, moral philosophy, geology, or anatomy, without exposing their faith or morals to imminent danger, unless a Roman Catholic professor will be appointed for each of those chairs.

"That if any president, vice-president, professor or office-bearer in any of the new Colleges, shall be convicted before the Board of Trustees, of attempting to undermine the faith or injure the morals of any student in those institutions, he shall be immediately removed from his office by the same Board.

"That as it is not contemplated that the students shall be provided with lodging in the new Colleges, there shall be a Roman Catholic chaplain to superintend the moral and religious instruction of the Roman Catholic students belonging to each of those Colleges; that the appointment of each chaplain, with a suitable salary, shall be made on the recommendation of the Roman Catholic Bishop of the diocese in which the College is situate, and that the same prelate shall have full power and authority to remove such Roman Catholic chaplain from his situation.

"Signed on behalf of the meeting,
"Marlborough St., Dublin,   "D. MURRAY, Chairman.
"May 23, 1845."

not grant the concessions asked for. The Bill, however, was passed. Archbishop Murray announced his intention of giving it a fair trial, and the Bishops of Cork, Belfast, and Galway adopted the same course.

Other prelates were unflinching in their opposition to the new system. The *Tablet*, under the able and vigorous editorship of Lucas, wrote with considerable vehemence in support of the latter party. After a long and rather heated controversy, the question was referred to Rome, but the final decision did not arrive till October, 1847. It was unfavourable to the Colleges, though it did not actually forbid them to Catholic students. But the question was now practically settled, and a few years later the prelates of Ireland legislated in detail on the points connected with these Colleges, and on which the Roman Congregation had only laid down the general lines to be followed.

In 1852, a great national synod was held at Thurles, and among other important matters, the question of attendance at the lectures of the Queen's University, and of the tenure of positions of authority in it, came on for discussion. The synod did not indeed prohibit young Catholics from studying there, nor were the positions of emolument altogether closed to Catholics, but the one and the other were so seriously discouraged, as to strike a blow that was practically fatal to the employment of the Colleges of the Queen's University by Catholics at large as a place of higher education for their children. No priest was allowed to hold any position there; no ecclesiastical student could study there, and all priests were forbidden to recommend it as a place of education to the faithful committed to their care. This decision was regarded at the time by many in Ireland, both priests and laymen, as a narrow and mistaken one; but as years passed on and the Catholic instinct of the nation rose superior to the natural feeling of disappointed expectation and personal judgment set aside, that warped the judgment of many at the first, the almost unanimous voice of the faithful confirmed the verdict of their prelates. From then till now the presence of Catholic students at the Queen's Colleges has been tolerated, but never sanctioned or approved by authority, and though a certain number of students have always availed themselves of the substantial advantages that they offer, yet the number is scarcely an appreciable one, with the single exception of the medical school of Cork. This school has won for itself a well-deserved reputation for the excellence of its teaching, and as the subject of medicine is one of those into which religious teaching very remotely enters, we do not suppose that any serious hindrance is placed to the presence of Catholic students in its lecture-rooms and laboratories.

The rapid glance that we have cast over the course of the higher education available to Catholic Ireland in the past, leads us on to the practical question of its present condition. Our object is to compare together the educational advantages possessed by Catholics with those that are in the possession of their Protestant fellow-subjects. We shall reckon up as fairly as we can, the revenues of the various Universities and University Colleges, which are essentially Protestant in their tone and character, or are absolutely secular and undenominational. To the former class belong Trinity College and the Queen's Colleges. These are, as we have shown, practically inaccessible to the generality of Catholics. But even here, in order that we may avoid all possible suspicion of unfairness in our calculations, we shall make a point of under-estimating the full value of the Protestant endowments, that the questionable benefit enjoyed by a handful of Catholics of sharing in the education at Trinity or the Queen's Colleges may not be alleged as vitiating our statistics.

The Royal University, which has already done so much for education in Ireland, will not enter into our calculations at all. We are dealing with teaching bodies, and the office of teacher does not form part of the functions assigned to the Royal University. Its business is to see that the work of instruction is properly done, not itself to do it. It resembles the London University in this, that it is a corporate body which only takes cognizance of knowledge already acquired, and does not directly aid the student in the acquiring of it. It requires no residence in this place rather than in that as a qualification for its degrees. It has no professors of its own, no Colleges forming integral parts of it, no endowment for teaching, except inasmuch as it makes it a condition of the Fellowships in connection with it that those who hold them shall, if required by the Senate, give their services in teaching students of the University in some educational institution approved by the Senate wherein matriculated students of the University are being taught. It has indeed certain Colleges attached to it. Of these there are the three Queen's Colleges already mentioned, the salaries of whose professors are in some instances increased by their election to Fellowships in the Royal University. A fourth is the Magee Presbyterian College at Londonderry. The fifth College is a Catholic College, and the appointment of some of its professors to Fellowships is the first step in the direction of the endowment of Catholic University Education. We shall return to this subject presently, in calculating the respective endowments of Protestant and Catholic Colleges in Ireland. But it does not affect the essential character of the Royal University as what is called an "essentially unsectarian body," and it merely puts a small number of Catholic professors on a par with their Protestant colleagues in the Queen's Colleges.

Our statement of the revenues of the various endowed Colleges of Ireland naturally commences with Trinity. Trinity is really only a College under the University of Dublin. But the latter body is at present in practice identical with its solitary College, or at all events, Trinity enjoys a monopoly of the privileges of the University to which it is attached. The income of the College is derived partly from external and partly from internal sources. Its external income consists mainly of rents derived from lands granted to it by the Crown. These lands are the property of the Monastery of All Hallows, confiscated by Elizabeth, and those of various recusants in the reign of James the First. The College has also an estate bestowed upon it by the Corporation of Dublin, and another bequeathed to it not long since by one of its former Provosts. Its internal income is that which is derived from the rental of the rooms let to students, the fees paid by them, &c. In the year 1866, according to a Parliamentary return the external and internal revenues of the College were as follows:

	NET RENTAL OF
1. EXTERNAL REVENUE:	ESTATES GRANTED.
	£ s. d.
By Queen Elizabeth and King James I.	31,369 19 8
Net rental from other sources - -	5,268 7 0
Dividends from Government Stock - -	885 13 10
Total - - - - -	37,524 0 6

2. INTERNAL REVENUE:

	£	s.	d.
Fees paid by Students	11,832	18	9
Fees on Degrees	2,731	7	0
Registration of University Electors & Fines	552	7	4
Net Rental of College Chambers	1,026	10	9
Total	16,143	3	10

We are going to confine ourselves to the external revenues of the College; but at the same time we must remind our readers that these do not at all exhaust its educational endowments. The house set aside for the Head, and justly termed his "palace;" the magnificent buildings where the Fellows live rent free; the spacious lecture-rooms and laboratories; the rooms occupied by students, which bring in a net income of over £1,000; and the wide acres of gardens and of park, in the very heart of the city, and compelling the unhappy traveller to make a long and tedious detour, as he seeks to pass from the north to the south of Dublin,—all these represent a noble sum of money, which ought to be reckoned in as part of the royal gifts still enjoyed by Trinity at the hand of the bounteous monarchs who set up this bulwark of Protestant orthodoxy.

But we will pass these over, because it is our intention throughout to underestimate rather than to exaggerate the educational endowments of Irish Protestants. At the same time it is but right that the reader should not forget that the nominal income of such an institution as Trinity is something very different from the full value of the unearned benefits that accrue to those who have the good fortune to find a place within its sacred precincts.

In 1875 a Parliamentary return similar to the preceding, places the external income of the College at £43,000, and we do not believe that we should be wrong in reckoning it at a still higher figure at the present day. But on the principle that we have adopted, we will put it at the round numbers of £40,000, and will take no account of the yearly value represented by its buildings, or of the actual payment received from the occupants of its rooms, or of the divers allowances, and stipends for offices almost or entirely nominal, or other pickings such as are prone to find their way into the pockets of all resident Fellows of such a College as Trinity.

The educational work done by it in return for its endowment is the education each year of some nine hundred Protestants, and some seventy Catholics. Of these, about half are non-resident. Most of them live in Dublin and merely attend Lectures at Trinity. There is another class whom it does not educate, but simply examines, in the same manner as the Royal University, or the University of London. But we understand that the number of these is inconsiderable, and that some eight hundred or nine hundred students, nearly all of them Protestant Episcopalians, receive their training, be it more or less, in return for the princely revenues with which Trinity is endowed and its splendid demesne in the midst of the Catholic city of Dublin.

From Trinity, which at least can boast a long prescription and traditions dating from three hundred years ago, we turn to the Queen's Colleges. They have existed only forty years, and cannot urge the intention of the founder as Trinity can. For the avowed object of the foundation of Trinity College was the subversion of the Catholic faith. It is true that Trinity can scarcely be said to claim Elizabeth as really its founder, since the funds employed for this object were simply the spoils of religious houses and of plundered Papists; and therefore her benevolent intentions need not count for much. But the Queen's Colleges, so far from being established in opposition to the Catholic faith, were designed for the relief of Catholic consciences, and as means of providing them with a University Education that they could conscientiously accept. Failing of this object, we may reasonably conclude that their founders would wish to see some rearrangement of their funds; and indeed the present English Government in proposing to make some change in them, is but carrying out the presumable intentions of those who held office in past years.

What then are the revenues of the three Queen's Colleges? Here we have the latest information in the Annual Report that the President of each of these Colleges has to send in year by year to the English Government. We will take the balance-sheets, contained in the Reports for the current year, as the basis of our calculation.

The official balance-sheet of these three Colleges shows a grant to each of them from Government of about £8,500, or in round numbers, of £25,000 to the combined three. Here, as in the case of Trinity, we purposely omit to calculate, as part of their yearly endowment, the substantial value of the lordly buildings with which the generosity of the Government has provided them. We simply reckon in the grant from the Consolidated Fund, and the further grant of £1,600 allotted to each in aid of maintenance.

With regard to these Colleges we have two questions

to consider: (1) Who are those who benefit educationally by these endowments? (2) How far is the work done by them at all proportionate to the income they receive?

From the Reports before us, we learn the religious denominations of those who are studying at them. Of these at Belfast there are 411 Protestants and 11 Catholics, 422 in all. At Galway, there are 71 Protestants and 36 Catholics, 107 in all. At Cork, there are 90 Protestants and 139 Catholics, or 229 in all. But here we must remark that of these 229 students, 162 are students in Medicine and only 41 students in Arts. Out of the 139 Catholic students, no less than 110 are students in Medicine and only 21 are students in the Faculty of Arts. Cork is in fact, as far as Catholics are concerned, almost entirely a medical school. At Galway also we find the Catholic students chiefly students in Medicine; out of the total of 38, only 13 being students in Arts. Of Belfast we have no information as to the respective numbers of Catholics in the two faculties, but the total of Catholics there is so small that the proportion is of no importance. If we suppose it to be the same as at the other two Colleges, we shall have, out of the total of 188 Catholics studying at them all, 152 who are medical students, and only 36 whose training is anything more than technical instruction which Catholics can receive in common with Protestants without any serious danger to faith or morals. In the only faculty which imparts education in the wider and truer sense in which it is distinguished from professional training, these three Colleges are practically non-existent, as far as Catholics are concerned. Common consent has stamped them as Protestant places of education, except as regards the medical schools of Cork. In all else they confer their benefits on the minority, consisting of one-fifth of the nation, and do little or nothing for those who form the remaining four-fifths.

Turning to the work they do in return for their munificent endowments, we must draw a very wide distinction, or rather a complete contrast between Belfast and the other two. Belfast College, situate in the midst of a population almost entirely Presbyterian, is for all practical purposes a denominational College. It is the chief educational institution in the whole of that flourishing and intelligent province. Provided with the best material in the sturdy youth of the North of Ireland, it turns to good advantage the mental vigour and moral force of the boys and young men it undertakes to train The universal testimony of those who differ most widely from the religious tenets of Presbyterianism, is that Belfast College not only employs its revenues in a way that gives it a solid claim to their continued enjoyment, but might with justice to its own claims, and with real benefit to the educational interests of Ireland, ask for some further grant from the English Government beyond that which it at present receives. We believe that almost every Catholic, who speaks either from acquaintance with the working of the College, or from a study of the brilliant and uniform successes it has achieved at the Royal University, would desire to see included in any scheme for the endowment of University Education in Ireland a provision for supplementing the endowment of Belfast College. It well deserves this, not only on account of the large number of its students, but also on account of its educational successes. It is not our task to reckon up the number of scholarships, prizes, and honours gained by it at the Royal University.

It is enough to say that it easily is well in advance, in this respect, of any other College throughout the length and breadth of the country.

The other two Queen's Colleges are in a very different position. We do not intend to impute any sort of blame to those who have the management of them. On the contrary, we believe that they have done all that could be done under the circumstances, to fulfil the design of those who founded them. It is not their fault that they are planted in the midst of a population who are unwilling and unable to avail themselves of the advantages they offer. It is not their fault if no satisfactory candidates offer themselves for the scholarships and prizes they have to offer, or if they do not achieve a very distinguished success. We do not expect them to make bricks without straw. We imagine that no one feels more acutely or so acutely the false position in which the Colleges of Galway and Cork are placed than the authorities of the Colleges themselves. It is always chilling and painful work for an able and energetic professor to have a class of three or four pupils of indifferent mental calibre, who perhaps are third-rate men from the active north, advised by their teachers to migrate to the west or south, in order to gain one of the scholarships which otherwise would go begging in Cork or Galway. Such a state of things ought to be put a stop to, in the interests of the learned men who at present waste their teaching powers on a class altogether unworthy of them, as well as in the interests of justice and sound learning, and of the intellectual advancement of the country at large.

What is the present state of Cork and Galway? We will take Cork first of all. It has 172 medical students, 41 students in the Faculty of Arts, 8 in Law, and 16 in

Engineering; 229 in all.[1] By far the larger portion of the endowments is assigned to the Faculty of Arts, and as it is this faculty which alone looks to intellectual cultivation, as distinguished from technical training, the small number of its art students compels us to regard the College as not having in any way fulfilled the primary object with which it was planted in the second city of Catholic Ireland. When moreover we turn to the results that it has to show, we must confess that they are sadly meagre. The number of exhibitions won by the College at Cork at the Royal University in a period extending over the last five years is 21. The number of honours gained by its students is 65.

The condition of Galway is still less satisfactory. It has at present 42 students in Medicine and 55 in Arts, 6 in Law, and 5 in Engineering; 107 in all. When tested by the results of examination it shows far worse results even than Cork. It obtains in the same period of five years only 11 exhibitions, and only 52 can claim honours.

In order to appreciate the bearing of these statistics, we must compare the successes of these two Colleges, with their rich endowments, amounting together to £20,000 a year, with the exhibitions and honours gained by the two unendowed Colleges of Blackrock and University College, Dublin, in the same period. The two Catholic Colleges have gained respectively 37 and 44 exhibitions, as compared with the 11 and 21 of the two Queen's Colleges, and contribute to the honour lists 118 and 168 names, as compared with the 52 and 65 of Cork and Galway. Thus the Catholic Colleges have together 81 exhibitions and 286 honours, as

[1] The apparent discrepancy in the figures arises from the fact that several are students in more than one faculty.

opposed to the 32 exhibitions and 117 honours of the two Queen's Colleges, or more than double under either head.[1]

Hitherto we have been making an estimate of the endowments provided for the higher education of those who form collectively one-fifth part of the whole population of the country. We now come to the endowments of which the remaining four-fifths have the opportunity of availing themselves. We have to see what *ought to be* done and what *is* done for the bulk of the population, in the land that justly bears the name of Catholic Ireland. In order to have due proportion, the educational endowments of a Catholic University, or of the various Catholic University Colleges, should, if we reckon mere numbers, be four times the endowments of the Protestant and undenominational Universities and Colleges. We should have to take the yearly income accruing to Trinity College from her wide domains, and the sum of the yearly grants enjoyed by the Queen's Colleges, and must multiply this total by four, in order to see what the Catholic population ought proportionately to receive. Even this, however, would still be to leave the Catholics at a disadvantage, unless they were also provided with commodious buildings, four times in extent the combined buildings of lordly Trinity, and with other buildings, either in the same spot, or in other parts of the country, which should represent a value four times that of the combined value of the handsome and well-appointed buildings of the three Queen's Colleges and

---

[1] We quote these statistics from the Archbishop of Dublin's address, delivered on November 8, 1889, at the Catholic University Medical School.

of all the convenient appliances that a generous Legislature has furnished to them. Nor is this all. Side by side with the princely estate of Royal Trinity there ought to spread out likewise in the heart of the city of Dublin, or at all events in some position or positions where it would be equally convenient, an estate or series of estates, of equal monetary value. Then, and not till then, should we have strict equality.

I quite allow that such a claim as this is one rather of theory than of any practical import at the present time. The poverty of Catholics, while it in one way gives them a greater claim to endowment than their richer Protestant neighbours, at the same time reduces those who are in fact capable of availing themselves of it to a minority of the population. To ask for the magnificent sum that the numerical proportion of Catholics to Protestants would give us, would be simply ridiculous. Yet if we suppose the injustice of the past undone, and calculate what would (as far as human foresight can judge) have been the relative conditions of the Catholic and Protestant population, every one must conclude that Protestants would have not been half as numerous as they at present are, and that Catholics would at least have been as much their equals in social position and early education as they are in active intelligence and eagerness to acquire knowledge. It is because the robbery and unscrupulous violence and oppression of Elizabeth and Cromwell and their successors have done their work only too well, that Protestants amount to a fifth part of the Irish population, and have so large a share of the wealth and refinement and culture and intellectual training that is to be found in Ireland. But even taking things as they are, the number of Catholics who are at the present moment able to avail themselves of University Education is larger than the number of Protestants. I shall prove this presently. I now merely anticipate the conclusion I shall then arrive at, in order that the present injustice may be the more clearly seen.

We now turn from the enumeration of the liberal endowments of Protestant University Education in Ireland to the other side of the picture. It will not detain us long. The muster-roll of the aids granted to Catholic Universities and Colleges consists of one solitary item, which we owe to the Senate of the Royal University, and which is not a direct grant at all to any Catholic University or College, but is simply an indirect and sidelong boon. It consists in the obligation attaching to certain members of the Royal University to devote some portion of their time to giving lectures in the Catholic University College of Dublin. This duty is by no means the only duty attaching to their office; we can scarcely call it their primary duty. They are Examiners as well as teachers, and the name given to those of them who have been recently appointed, and which was substituted for the former name of "Fellows," may be regarded as indicating the relative importance of their combined functions. They are called "Teaching Examiners." Their duty of examining is fixed and altogether independent of themselves, both in its duration, the amount of time to be devoted to it, and the seasons of the year when it occupies their attention. Their teaching duties are quite indefinite, and dependent in great measure on the will of the bearer of the office. The amount of lectures to be given is not fixed; they have to cease as soon as any examination begins. We are sure that the authorities of University College would bear grateful testimony to the services rendered by many of these gentlemen, but it is impossible to forget that every claim on them must depend in great measure on their individual devotedness, and that as Teaching Examiners they are bound to put, in the first place, their duty as Examiners, and only, in the second and subordinate place, their duty as teachers in the College to which they are attached. Outside this indirect and quasi-endowment, Catholic University Education receives absolutely nothing. However efficient the teaching, however distinguished the success attained by any College, no hand is stretched out to help its struggles to impart the advantages of the higher education and intellectual training to young Catholic Irishmen.

This contrast between *what ought to be* and *what is* deserves the close attention of all those who are interested in the now imminent question of *what is to be*.

What ought to be is this. Catholics ought to have at their disposal, if perfect equality is to be established, endowments for University Education corresponding to the amount of the Catholic as compared with the Protestant population of Ireland, who are able to avail themselves of it.

But the Catholics of Ireland who are able to avail themselves of University Education are, as I shall prove presently, more than half the population of the country.

Therefore the endowments of Catholic education in Ireland ought to be, in common justice, more than equal to the endowments of Protestant education.

What is may be stated as follows :

The endowments of Protestant education in Ireland consist of the endowments of Trinity and the endowments of the three Queen's Colleges. But the endowments of Trinity amount to £40,000 and more, and the endowments of the three Queen's Colleges amount to over £25,000. Therefore the total endowments of Protestant and godless education in Ireland amount to over £65,000. On the other hand, the endowments of Catholic education are absolutely nothing, unless indeed we reckon as an endowment the obligation of some dozen Fellows or Teaching Examiners of the Royal University, to add to their duties as Examiners the duty of lecturing in the Catholic University of Dublin.

Hence, while the endowments of one-fifth of the population amount to over £65,000, the endowment of the remaining four-fifths amounts at most to the paltry sum which is represented by the payment of thirteen Fellows of the Royal University to lecture in the Catholic University College of Dublin.

Such is the strange contrast between what ought to be and what is.

II.

THE question of University Education for the Catholics of Ireland is one that is at a certain disadvantage as compared with a number of other questions that are crying out for solution at the present time. It is only natural that the material and social needs of the country should be more prominently before the minds of men than its intellectual requirements. The settlement of the land question and the arrangement of some amicable *modus vivendi* between landlords and tenants, the promotion of the many Irish industries which only need encouragement and capital to revive and flourish, the remedy for the abject poverty of some portions of Western Ireland the development of the fisheries, the adoption of such means as may stop the gradual depopulation of the country districts,—all these are matters which to ordinary men seem of immeasureably greater importance than the endowment of the Higher Education of the Catholic youth of Ireland. They make more impression on the imagination; they appeal more to our natural sense of justice and love of country; they directly and immediately affect a far larger class, and a class of men less able to help themselves; they promise a more speedy relief; they deal with what seems more absolutely necessary to the well-being of the people than the Higher Education, which is regarded as benefiting only a few, and of comparatively small importance to the rank and file of the inhabitants of Ireland.

Hence it is that those who do not look far forward, and who forget the close connection that exists between intellectual and material progress, would have us put aside, at all events for a time, our demand for some large concession to the claims of Ireland in the matter of University Education. So, too, when famine prevails in some widespread district, and the scanty harvest yields but a few ears to the famished occupiers of the land, there are some who are satisfied if they can provide an immediate supply for the wants of the sufferers. But he who is prudent will look further. He will procure a large store of the best grain to be sown, with an eye to years to come, on the wasted plains. He will look to the manner of tillage, and to the instruction of the inhabitants in the due rotation of crops, in the use of suitable fertilizing materials, and in all else that is necessary to successful husbandry. Such a one will confer a more lasting benefit on the holders of those barren acres than those who look only to the supply of their immediate needs, and in years to come they will gratefully remember his far-sighted wisdom.

The social and moral condition of Ireland in many respects resembles that of some such district, where the soil, once fertile, has been rendered barren by blighting agencies that destroyed its fruitfulness. The parallel holds good in this respect among others, that those who desire to establish on a solid basis the future prosperity of their country, will regard as of primary importance in this crisis of her fortunes, the sowing of good seed and the adoption of a sound system of the Higher Education so as to produce in years to come a generation of Irishmen, trained in her own schools with the best intellectual and moral training within her reach, that thus they may go forth to fight the battle of life fully equipped, and ready to hold their own against all comers. How can Ireland expect her next generation of statesmen to take the wise and far-sighted and prudent view of all that is needed to heal their country's wounds and to renew her strength and vigour, if they are not versed in the principles that govern economic science and political development? How can she expect them to be close reasoners and logical thinkers, unless they are trained to exact and scientific thought? How can she expect her sons to take the place once more that they occupied of old in scholarship and classic lore, in bold philosophical speculation and in the tedious labour of historical research, unless they are taught by experience to appreciate the value of intellectual excellence? How are they to take the foremost place in the ranks of those who are clad in "sweetness and light," unless they drink in their youth at the Castalian spring; and court the company of the sacred Nine? It is true that there is in every class in Catholic Ireland a natural refinement that is independent of any artificial culture. It is true also that there are not a few who have attained brilliant successes in many a walk of life in spite of their having been debarred from the higher training. But such men are the exception, not the rule. It is not for men of extraordinary talent that we have to legislate. Genius, or a very remarkable talent, will under any circumstances push its way to the front. Such men ascend by rapid leaps where ordinary mortals clamber slowly and painfully up the ladder that leads to a high place in art or literature, in commerce and in politics, in the various learned professions that lead the way to influential positions in the commonwealth. It is to the class of men of an intelligence not much beyond the average that we have to look. We have to stimulate their energy, to help them to develope their mental powers, to encourage them in their praiseworthy ambition, to place within their reach means of cultivation to which access is denied them at present. We have to raise the general intellectual standard throughout the country, and in doing so we shall afford substantial benefits even to those whose native talent can overleap the obstacles that are prohibitory to others, and we shall moreover bring to the front rank many who but for the Higher Education would have remained all their lives through in some subordinate and inferior position.

We must also bear in mind that the work of Education must be done gradually. Nature will not be hurried in her noblest achievements. It is only when it has become a tradition of the country that a good system of education produces its full fruit. A good system cannot even be set on foot without many a preliminary process. "First the blade, then the ear, then the full corn in the ear." Nay, each separate stage of it must grow up slowly if it is to produce a ripe and an enduring harvest. We must begin, as we have begun in Ireland, with Primary Education ; we must go on, as we have gone on, to Intermediate Education ; and when at last we come to that higher culture that is to crown the edifice, we must still be content to arrive at our final results only by a gradual development. The foundations of the Higher Education have now been happily laid for us in that system of Examination (for it is little more) that we call the Royal University. The various Colleges that send up their students for its Examinations have for nine years past been striving, in spite of the crushing disadvantages of the traditions of the past and the poverty of the present, to set on foot an organized system of efficient teaching and discipline. It now remains to fill up the framework with an endowed system of teaching, that shall freely distribute to those who hunger for it, but hitherto have been unable to satisfy their longing, the wholesome food of solid learning.

But we must not expect to be able to bring into existence a perfect system as Athene sprang in all her panoply from the head of Zeus. We might have the amplest revenues; we might have a College or a University completely equipped and endowed in every faculty; we might have buildings grander than those of Galway and Cork. We might have Fellowships as rich as the best Fellowships of Trinity; we might have grounds and playing-fields as spacious as those which stretch away in the centre of Dublin city; yet all this would be of little value unless there simultaneously grew up a gradual process of intellectual construction, developing in the sons and daughters of Catholic Ireland the knowledge and scholarship, the thirst for knowledge, and the eager intellectual ambition, of which the complete system is the coping-stone and the crown. Remembering all this, we see at once how mistaken is the view of those who would have us postpone the question of University Education until such time as Ireland may be at liberty to inaugurate a system which may offer to her children in all completeness and perfection the opportunities of mental cultivation. When that day comes, the solution of the educational problem will not be at all the simplest of the questions that will have to be solved. It will require that those to whom it is submitted should be not only earnest lovers of their country, and ready to promote her welfare without any thought of personal advantage or any desire to gain a party victory. It will not be enough that they should be men of intelligence and wisdom, practised in the affairs of State, with a keen appreciation of all that may promote their country's good. It will not be enough that they should be good financiers and economists, ready to vote large sums with far-sighted generosity for any object that will promote the welfare of Ireland. All this they must be, but they must be something more. They must also have among them those whose own training has been of the highest kind. There must be those who have watched the fortunes of the system that has been gradually growing up in Ireland, and supplying the needs of her children. There must be those who are competent to pronounce judgment on the respective claims of a classical, mathematical, and scientific training. There must be those who have a solid opinion as to the stage when general education is to be exchanged for professional or technical instruction. There must be men not only of intelligence, but of trained, and highly trained, intelligence. How are we to have all this if, forsooth, we are to refuse the offers made us at the present time, offers which, we hope and believe, will be made in no grudging or niggardly spirit, but with a sincere desire to satisfy our just claims to educational equality with our Protestant fellow-countrymen?

The element of wisdom that underlies this proposal of postponement is to be found in the conviction that any system of endowment that may be inaugurated now cannot be final. It can be but a step in the right direction, and must be accepted as such. What

Catholics have a right to receive is perfect equality with their Protestant neighbours in the endowments granted them for the promotion of University Education. This equality must at the present time be a relative and provisional, rather than an absolute equality. It must be an equality of principle, rather than one of positive fact. For if by equality is meant an endowment proportionate in amount to the ratio of the Catholic and Protestant population, the endowment which Catholics claim would be an annual sum of not more than a quarter of a million, supposing always that the endowments at present in the hands of Protestants remain untouched. To demand such a sum as this would be, as I have already remarked, obviously absurd. If we asked for it we should not get it, and should moreover deserve to be regarded as "Intransigeants," and to be sent away empty-handed. Even if it were granted us, we should scarcely know how to expend so large a sum on University Education, and there would be a considerable danger that it would prove a fatal, or at least a very unmanageable, gift. To take equality, on the other hand, to mean an absolute equality is to assume a purely arbitrary standard. To allot exactly the same amount to one-fifth as to four-fifths of the population is clearly no equality at all, or would at all events only be a real equality on the supposition that among the four-fifths of the population there were only the same number of persons capable of profiting by the higher training as among the remaining one-fifth.

This suggests a further question, which is one of no small importance in its bearing on the amount of endowment that Irish Catholics are entitled to for purposes of University Education. It is useless to offer a boon unless the recipients are in a condition to avail themselves of it. How far is the intellectual and social condition of Catholic Ireland one that enables her children to employ it profitably? It used to be said before the Royal University was set on foot, that all the Catholics who had any desire for intellectual advancement were already provided for. Some of them went to Trinity, others to the Queen's Colleges, while those who had a conscientious objection to both the one and the other, were sent to France or Belgium, or to some College in England, where some mental training beyond an ordinary school course may be obtained, these last, however, being too small a class to be worth taking into account. Outside of these, it was said that there were practically no Catholics who had any intellectual aspirations such as a University is intended to supply.

This sort of talk was silenced once and for ever by the large and continually increasing numbers that have availed themselves of the Intermediate Education Act, and of the Examinations of the Royal University. In spite of the sedulous care with which, for centuries, intellectual cultivation was absolutely forbidden to Catholics, except at the price of apostacy—in spite of painful illiteracy to which Catholic Ireland has had to submit, and which is in one sense her glory, because it is one of the many scars which tell of her victory over all the base and futile attempts to rob her of the priceless treasure of her Faith—in spite of the well-endowed and well-appointed schools which gave to the Protestants of the country an almost irresistible superiority over the unaided efforts of their Catholic fellow-subjects—in spite of past traditions, in spite of present poverty, in spite of the apparent hopelessness of their efforts with such overwhelming odds against them, the Catholic youth of Ireland have come forward from every class, from every quarter of the country, from every Catholic school or College of Higher Education, and in the face of all these disadvantages have distanced their Protestant competitors in every stage of the Examinations held under the Intermediate Education Act, and are now beginning to run them close even in the Examinations of the Royal University.

It is true that in the latter, one institution which is virtually, if not nominally, a Presbyterian place of education, has hitherto surpassed all rivals, whether Catholics or Protestants, both in the number of passes, and of Exhibitions and Honours gained. No College of any size can show such results in the shape of University distinctions, as Queen's College, Belfast. No Catholic will grudge it its well-deserved success. It is an example that we shall do well to imitate. But I am sure that Belfast College would be the first to recognize the disadvantages under which Catholic Colleges labour as compared with it, and how their friendly battle with it is the battle of a mere recent and ill-armed levy with a well-trained army, which has the newest and most scientific weapons in its hands. Belfast College is situated in the midst of a population, whose strong intelligence has for long years past been strengthened and stimulated by unceasing aid and encouragement from the English Government. While the industries of the rest of Ireland were crushed out by laws virtually, and often actually, prohibitive, favoured Ulster was made an exception to the oppressive enactments.

Thus enabled to develope her trade, Ulster continually advanced in prosperity and wealth. This made a thorough education more and more within the reach of all her citizens, and enabled them to appreciate its importance. The schools of Secondary Education in Ulster are consequently of first-class quality. They are able to offer inducements to the best teachers among the Protestants of Ireland to come and teach in them, and the material on which they have to work is of a corresponding character. The Ulster boys are many of them of Scottish extraction, or the children of mixed parentage, who combine the perseverance and hard-headedness of the Scot with the bright intelligence and quickness of apprehension that mark the Celt. These natural gifts, combined with the adventitious advantages that the Protestants of Ireland have enjoyed for centuries, and with the consequent prosperity and wealth of the North, give to Belfast College every chance of success. And when we add to all this the endowment it enjoys, an endowment which we believe to be insufficient, but which nevertheless gives it an immense advantage over the unendowed Colleges of Catholics, can we wonder that hitherto Belfast has carried off the largest share in the honours and prizes in the Royal University? We do not mean to allow this state of things to continue: year by year Catholics are gaining and will gain on their Protestant competitors. But how can they expect to run an even race while they are mercilessly handicapped by the entire absence of those material resources which are indispensable to the highest education in the present day?

Even when those resources are granted, we cannot expect Catholic Ireland to come forward at once with the love of learning for its own sake fully developed, or to shake itself free from the traditions of ignorance and illiteracy to which it was condemned for centuries.

We cannot look for a full appreciation of the importance of the higher training from those whose ancestors were forced by penal laws to abstain from any sort of Catholic education, and so came to regard it as something outside the range of practical politics. But the longing for education has never been extinguished; it smouldered beneath the surface during the long time of bondage, and only needed freedom and encouragement to break into a flame at any moment. Freedom, through God's mercy, is now the lot of the Higher Education of Ireland; it has, moreover, already received an instalment of the encouragement necessary for its full development, and now it has, or seems to have, the promise of a liberal and generous endowment before many months are past. But before we speak of generosity, we must see what is required by justice.

The Catholics of Ireland have at least a right of justice to a perfect equality with their Protestant fellow-subjects. They have, if anything, a claim to even a more liberal treatment by reason of the hardships of the past. If a mother had two children and had shown herself in the case of one of them not only a harsh but a cruel and unnatural parent, if she had for years starved her unhappy offspring, and torn from it the very nourishment that it had sought elsewhere, if she had bestowed on its favoured brother the food that belonged of right to the poor starveling, and had indeed done her best to destroy its life altogether—in such a case as this, would not the mother, when at length she returns to a better mind, be bound to try and compensate the sufferer by extra generosity, and by giving it not only the same nutritious diet that its favoured brother has enjoyed, but even something in addition to make up for the injustice inflicted upon it? So, too, Catholics in Ireland have a right to look for liberal terms in this matter of the Higher Education. Such liberality should be called justice rather than generosity. It is the least that can be done to obliterate the memory of the painful past.

I ask the reader to bear this in mind as he reads the very moderate claims that Catholics advance in this matter. All that they ask for is bare equality with Protestants. Such equality includes not merely equality of revenues, for these are but one element in view of future efficiency. There must be in addition to this, equality of prestige (so far as it is possible to ensure it), and also equality in buildings, position, facilities of teaching, and all else that contributes to the success in the work that a University has to do. I have already spoken of the difficulty of determining what equality of endowment really means. It is impossible to do more than state what might be considered a fair basis on which to make the calculation.

I do not think that any endowment would be considered equitable which did not at the very least provide for Catholics in the same proportion to Protestants, as there are at the present time Catholic boys whose previous education has been tested by results, and has shown them to be fully qualified for the further education that is given at a University. Such a test is fortunately given in the Intermediate Examinations, which practically include every boy of promise whether Catholic or Protestant, who has passed successfully through the best schools throughout the country. In these Examinations all (or almost all) the boys present themselves who afterwards distinguish themselves at Trinity College, all the boys who take the best places in the Royal University, all who intend to enter on any of the learned professions, and many more beside. If in these Examinations the Catholics were distanced by Protestants, then they would scarcely be able to claim at present an endowment for their further education equal to that of Protestants. But if, in spite of all the various drawbacks to their education in the past and the disadvantages they are still under even in the present, they more than hold their own against their more fortunate brethren, if there are more Catholics than Protestants whose intellectual attainments at the end of their school course show them to be able to reap the benefits of University Education, if the numbers of Catholics who pass the Intermediate Examination is larger than the number of Protestants, if the best places and greater share in the prizes and scholarships fall to the lot of Catholics, then I think no one can in any fairness refuse them the same substantial aid in the higher training which is already enjoyed by the happy denizens of Trinity College and other places of education which are at present practically closed to Catholics.

In making our calculation I shall confine myself to the senior and middle grades. They give a result less favourable to the claims of Catholics than the junior grade. In so doing I was not sure that my estimate is quite fair. There are a large number of Catholic boys who are successful in the junior grade, and who are only prevented by poverty from pursuing their education to the end of the school course and passing then to the University. Such boys would often appear in the lists of the middle and senior grades if they had before them the prospect of a University Education on such easy terms as open out to Protestant boys, with a far-off vista of still greater academic or literary or professional success in the far future. But we must be satisfied to take simply the results of the two higher grades. I will take the numbers of the Catholics and Protestants respectively who have passed the middle and the senior grades during the last three years. By a comparison of these we shall be able to form a fair notion of the proportion of the Catholics and Protestants who are intellectually qualified to receive a University Education. This will furnish a direct means of estimating the proportionate endowment which ought to be assigned to these two respective classes of the community for the purposes of University Education; or rather, I should say, thence we shall be able to estimate the minimum of endowment which Catholics can justly claim. I have already remarked that the long educational injustice of the past reduces to a level of ordinary justice, or at least of equity, treatment which would otherwise be generous. But this is not all. The mere poverty of Catholics, quite apart from their past educational disabilities, gives them a greater claim than their far wealthier neighbours. Take the case of two boys of equal ability, one a Catholic and the other a Protestant. They have obtained the same marks in the senior grade of the Intermediate Examination. I will suppose them equal in perseverance, virtue, and energy. But the Protestant is well to do, the Catholic is poor, not from any fault of his own, but simply because in trade and in the professions alike Protestants have lived under the smile of a paternal Government, whereas Catholics have struggled on as best they could under discouragement and neglect, if not persecution, for centuries. Has not the Catholic a claim to something more than equal treatment as compared with his more wealthy and favoured brother?

But there is another reason why Catholics have a claim to something more. The figures I am going to adduce do not indicate the full claim that Catholics may justly make, if the settlement is to be fixed for years to come as well as to decide merely what is to be allotted them for the current year. For the statistics of the Examinations point to a steady advance of Catholics in their qualification for University Education. The percentage of Catholics to Protestants has regularly increased in every grade of the Intermediate Examinations. Year by year, with scarcely an exception, they have gained on the Protestants. Thus in the year 1879 the Catholics who passed the two higher grades were in a distinct minority, 247 to 404 Protestants. In 1881 they were neck and neck, 393 to 410. In the following year they were slightly ahead, 401 to 386, and in the year 1887 they were very considerably superior to their opponents, 332 to 278.[1]

[1] Our readers may be interested to know the respective numbers from Catholic and Protestant schools who have passed the middle and senior grades of the Intermediate Examinations, in each several year from 1879 to 1887.

TABLE 1.
Numbers for the several years from 1879 to 1887:

Year	Catholics	Protestants	Percentage of Catholics
1879.	247.	404.	37·9.
1880.	355.	409.	46·5.
1881.	393.	410.	48·9.
1882.	401.	386.	50·9.
1883.	416.	322.	56·3.
1884.	340.	304.	52·7.
1885.	317.	230.	58·0.
1886.	345.	261.	56·9.
1887.	332.	278.	54·4.

TABLE 2.
Numbers for periods of three years from 1879 to 1887:

Period	Catholics	Protestants	Percent. of Catholics
1879 to 1881.	995.	1223.	45·0.
1882 to 1884.	1157.	1012.	53·3.
1885 to 1887.	994.	769.	56·3.

Now, supposing the same progress to continue, in a few years the Catholics will completely distance the Protestants, even supposing them to be still seriously prejudiced, as they are now, by reason of the absence of educational endowments. If, however, they should receive at least some portion of the aid that they can numerically claim, we may look forward to their numbers being before long the double of those of Protestants. They are sure to double them, and they ought to double them, with a population four times as great, and though we cannot expect endowments to be given to Catholics in view of what they hope and expect to be, but only in view of what at present they are, yet the prospect of increase is a reason for a large and generous treatment of those who amount to four-fifths of the population of Ireland.

I now come to apply my figures. During the last three years the total number of Catholics who passed the two higher grades of the Intermediate Examinations was 994, the total number of Protestants 769. Catholics were thus 56·3 per cent. of the whole number,

As our figures were obtained by adding together those who have passed middle and senior grades in different years, we necessarily count a certain number twice over, but this does not materially affect the proportionate results.

There is one feature in the statistics of the Intermediate Examination which we omit in our text for simplicity's sake, but which deserves special attention. While the percentage of Catholics, as compared with Protestants, who pass the two higher grades of the Intermediate Examination about fifty-six per cent., the percentage of those who obtain Honours is about sixty-five per cent. This is a very remarkable fact, showing clearly that among those who present themselves for these Examinations, there is a far higher attainment and more talent and promise among Catholics than among Protestants. A difference of nearly ten per cent. in favour of the former in percentage means a difference of some twenty per cent. between the two classes when compared together. Bearing always in mind the advantages enjoyed by Protestants in the facilities for education and in the endowments which they are able to devote to pushing on their most promising boys, this fact speaks volumes.

E

and Protestants 43·7, or about 14 to 11. The proportion of those who obtained Honours during the same period was nearly 65 per cent., or about 14 Catholics to 8 Protestants. Taking these numbers to represent, as they very fairly do, the proportion of claimants for aid in University Education, we are able to calculate what that aid should be. Supposing the endowments of Protestants to remain as at present, some £65,000, the endowment which Catholics can claim on grounds of strict equality, will be a minimum of £80,000. In other words, if £65,000 is the sum which can at the present be expended with advantage by the State on stimulating the intellectual advancement of the Protestant youth of Ireland, the sum which bare justice would allot to the Catholic youth of the country for the same purpose will be over £80,000.

I leave these figures to speak for themselves. They are calculated, as we have shown, with a leaning to cut down the Catholic claims as much as possible. I have minimized the existing endowments. I have minimized the Catholic claims. Yet in spite of all this minimizing, the barest justice, the lowest notion that can be taken of equality of endowment, would give to Catholics a yearly grant of more than £80,000, always supposing the Protestant endowments to remain as at present. They take no account of the steady advance in their intellectual superiority even under their present disadvantages.

But a mere money equality is not all that Irish Catholics have a right to demand in this matter of University Education. It would avail them little to have rich endowments, so long as they are denied the social and intellectual prestige that has been hitherto the monopoly of Protestants, and more especially of those Protestants who belong to the comparatively small class of Episcopalians in Ireland. For it is well for us to remember that although in many respects the Presbyterians of Ulster have been the spoilt children of the Cromwellian settlement of the country, and of those on whom the mantle of Cromwell fell, yet in the matter of education they have been in a very distinct position of inferiority. Trinity College, with its magnificent endowments was practically closed (or almost closed) to them until Mr. Fawcett's Bill abolished the restrictions that shut them out from all the emoluments of that institution. Even now they frequent it but little. It still remains the stay and support of the Episcopalian Church alone. Its revenues are very effective in neutralizing the prejudicial effect that the disendowment of the Irish Church would otherwise have had on its social status. As long as Trinity maintains its exclusive position, so long will a sort of moral and social superiority cling to the Episcopalian body.

I do not say this from any hostility to Protestant Episcopalianism. Trinity is in a religious position distinctly superior to that of Colleges where no sort of religion is recognized. But I cannot regard the exclusiveness of the position that Trinity occupies as at all consistent with any possible theory of religious equality. It is not that Catholics grudge it its revenues. It is not that we do not appreciate the valuable work that it has done and is still doing. It is not that we forget the number of distinguished men that it has produced, or those who are at the present time to be found among its Fellows. We do not desire to interfere with it in any way, except in this single matter of the exclusiveness of its tenure. Representing as it does only an eighth or tenth portion of the population of Ireland, representing only a minority of the talent of the country, it cannot be fair that it should remain the sole representative of the various Colleges which ought to be grouped together under one common University, and what is more, that it should be in the general estimation of mankind, identical in practice if not in theory, with the teaching University of Ireland. It is confessedly in a false position, and a false position is sooner or later fatal to the well-being of any institution. Even for its own sake Trinity ought to be brought into its proper relation to the other teaching Colleges of Ireland. It should be one of a group, all united, as was the intention of its founders, under one common University. For Trinity is in theory, and was originally meant to be, a College subordinate to the University of Dublin. It is the University, not the College, that in theory examines and confers degrees. In the statutes of the University provision is made for the foundation of other Colleges under its mantle besides Trinity. All that is needed is to make this provision a reality. Leave Trinity by all means in its present splendid position as a College, but admit side by side with it other Colleges under one common University. Whether this common University be called the University of Dublin or the Royal University of Ireland, matters but little.[1] What is essential is that a Catholic College (and for the matter of that, a Presbyterian College also) should be admitted on equal terms to rank side by side with, though separate from, Trinity College, as Colleges of a common University which shall include them all. Whether the Presby-

[1] The Royal University of Ireland is the more appropriate title, as indicating the University of the whole nation, and not of one town or district.

terian body would wish to have their main teaching centre in Dublin or Belfast is a question that does not concern us. We only allude to their claims because we are advocating the due recognition of various religious bodies to endowment in relation to the secular teaching that they give to their own co-religionists. This is all that Catholics claim for the Catholic body, and this we would on the principle of even-handed justice desire to see given to Presbyterians also.

I repeat then that what Catholics and Presbyterians have a right to is this—that under a common University (whether that University be called the Royal University of Ireland or the University of Dublin), there should be included on terms of perfect equality a Catholic College and a Presbyterian College, in addition to the Episcopalian College of Trinity, which at present enjoys a most unjust monopoly.

This introduces the question (and it is one on which a great deal of misapprehension exists among Protestants), as to the endowment of Colleges which make the theological teaching a part of their programme, and more particularly the endowment of professorial chairs directly or indirectly established for the imparting of certain theological opinions. Protestants seem to fancy that the Catholic body in Ireland, and especially the Bishops, are determined by hook or by crook to divert the endowments they may receive for controversial and propagandist purposes. It is perhaps a natural and reasonable mistake for those who are not Catholics to make, and it is one that bears unconscious testimony to the supremacy which would be given to theology as the science of all sciences, the queen and mistress of all the rest, in an ideal University. But Universities are not ideal in the present day, and we imagine never will be as long as the world shall last. The days are past when the names still painted over the antique doors in the Schools quadrangle at Oxford have any real significance. There was, indeed, a period when "Schola Ethicæ," "Schola Metaphysicæ," "Schola Naturalis Philosophiæ," "Schola Theologiæ," really indicated the character of the sciences taught within. But that period is a matter of history, not only for Protestant Oxford, but also for Catholic Ireland, at all events under present circumstances. We are concerned with what is possible in the existing state of things, not with what might be possible in an imaginary condition of the world around us.

But even in an ideal University, unless indeed it made express provision for the complete training of students for the priesthood, we are not so sure that there ought to be any endowment for Theology or Theological Chairs. Theology is not, and never was, a part of the literal education of laymen. In the middle ages their training stopped short at philosophy, none save clerics proceeded to the study of theology. The general consensus of Catholic opinion is in favour of an education apart for the young cleric who is studying his Theology when the common training which he shared with the lay students around is over. Maynooth and Clonliffe and the various diocesan seminaries throughout the country would never consent to send their theologians to study theology at a Catholic University College, and a Catholic College would find their presence within its walls unsuitable. A theological faculty would have very few students to follow its lectures. It is quite different in a Protestant University where the secular learning is not only the predominant but the almost conclusive feature of the training of

Protestant clergymen, and where the theological school, if it exists at all, is quite subordinate to the other branches of learning. But the divine science of theology is not one that in any way belongs to a liberal education. It is professional, technical, special, and its one aim is to equip the soldier of Christ with the weapons belonging to his sacred calling and to prepare him for a life different from any other life—a life which is or ought to be a "hidden life," a life apart, a life of prayer and retirement, and a sort of isolation so far as is possible consistent with his duties to the busy world in which he has to live.

It often appears to me that there was a strange inconsistency in the endowment of the Theological College of Maynooth by a Protestant Government, and that its disendowment was a very proper step for those who did not believe in the faith of the Catholic Church. No man could reasonably expect or wish a Protestant Government to pay money for the strengthening and building up of opinions that it regards with dislike and contempt, and we quite agree with the repudiation of any such idea by all reasonable men. We would almost go further and join our voice to the chorus of protest that arose against the very notion of Chairs of Theology or Ecclesiastical History being endowed from public funds. In Primary Education the endowment of denominational schools does not mean the endowment of denominational teaching, but on the contrary, expressly provides that none of the public money shall be devoted to promote any one set of religious opinions rather than another. So the endowment of Colleges, be they Catholic or Protestant, under a common and neutral University, does not mean that Catholic or Protestant Chairs of Theology or Ecclesiastical History should be endowed, but on the contrary, the measure passed should contain an express provision corresponding to that imposed on primary schools.

But in this we have a right to claim that the limitation placed on any grant made to Catholics should be extended to other religious bodies as well. It would be a strange sort of equality if the Catholic theologian were silenced, while the Protestant controversialist hard by were to receive a goodly sum to abuse "Romanists," and denounce the Pope, and to employ the authority of a dignified position to indoctrinate his pupils with the oft-refuted slanders which form the staple of the dogmatic teaching of the Protestant theologian of Ireland. Just as it was fair that Maynooth should cease to receive its yearly grant when the Irish Establishment was destroyed, so even-handed justice, in refusing, and very properly refusing, any endowment to Catholic theology, must also refuse to allow any public endowment to be attached to the teaching of any religious opinions outside the Catholic body. Without this there would not be real equality.

But here I must introduce a necessary proviso. It is one again to which those who have to legislate for us fancy that we shall not willingly submit. If in any Denominational College there are any students belonging to a denomination different from that to which the College belongs, such a student ought in every case to be exempted from attendance at any religious service, or instruction, or lecture to which he has a *bonâ fide* objection on religious grounds. He ought to be at no sort of disadvantage by reason of his religious opinions, and should be perfectly free to follow out in all respects the dictates of his conscience. In other words, every Denominational College must have a Conscience-clause strictly and impartially enforced. Any one who knows anything of the working of a Catholic College will know that such a clause will be practically unnecessary. To force those who are not Catholics to attendance on any occasion when they would be exposed to hear or see what would be inconsistent with what they regard as true, is utterly at variance with Catholic principles. At the University College in Stephen's Green there have always been a little knot of Protestant students. We are perfectly certain that if they were asked whether there had been any sort of interference with their convictions, or anything whatever to which they had a conscientious objection during the time that they were inmates of the College or attending its lectures, they would one and all bear willing testimony to the entire absence of the very faintest approach either to proselytism or to the enforcement of any kind of religious disability. The notion that Catholics seek to thrust their faith on outsiders is a pure invention of those who judge not from what they know to be the case, but from their antecedent and *a priori* notions of what they think must be the case. It is a charge that will not bear the light of day.

The very insertion in the charter of a Catholic College of a Conscience-clause is a harmless formality, though at the same time it is an uncalled-for reflection on the Catholic body. It is but another instance of that strange tendency of human nature to read in the character of our neighbours the faults to which we ourselves are prone.

For centuries there has been practised in Catholic Ireland a system of proselytism almost without a parallel. What means can be found that have not been employed to rob Ireland's children of their faith?

Persecution more cruel than that of Pagan Rome; kidnapping more shameless than that of the African slave-trader; bribery more utterly unprincipled than that of the most venal of Turkish officials; violence worthy of the brutality and lust of an Eastern despot; trickery, deceit, lying that would put to shame even the father of lies himself. Perhaps we cannot wonder that those whose hands have been defiled with such methods as these, from the lordly dignitary of Anglicanism to the miserable hireling who has made the sacred name of "Scripture reader" a synonym for all that is vile and contemptible—we cannot wonder that such men should suspect those whom they have vainly sought to seduce from virtue and from God, of a desire, now that the tide has turned, to practise some sort of retaliation. We will not grudge them the needless and innocuous Conscience-clause. If the landlord of a house, whose ancestors were notorious freebooters, were to insert in the lease that the tenant must engage not to appropriate his neighbour's goods, an honest man would smile at the uncomplimentary condition, but he would be willing enough that it should stand as a part of a beneficial lease offered him on generous terms.

I might apply the same principles of interpretation to another condition that which we are told is to be comprised in the grant to a University College for Catholics in Ireland. It is not to be used as a focus of sedition or as a means of disseminating political opinions hostile to the Government. This is a perfectly fair and just condition, and one which will be most readily accepted by Catholic Ireland. It does not mean that those who were before opposed to the policy of the party in power should henceforward support it, or should even regard it more favourably than they have hitherto done. It does not mean that the authorities of the new College should be understood to use their influence to induce the students under their care to adhere to a set of principles that they have hitherto regarded with aversion. It does not mean that the acceptance of it is to have any political influence whatever. If this were the condition imposed, every lover of his country, nay, every honest man in Ireland would repudiate even the richest endowment as nothing better than a traitor's bribe. But it does mean that there is to be perfect impartiality in matters political. The University College, as such, though it is to be denominational in religion, is not to be denominational in politics. The Professor of History is not to give a one-sided view of the past for his own purposes. The Professor of Political Economy is to exercise no undue influence when he has to deal with the industries of a country and the best means of promoting them. The Professor of Ethics is to hold the balance evenly in discussing questions respecting Government. All this is perfectly right, and we ought to welcome it as a boon to the Catholic cause in Ireland. What else do we need but the bare truth respecting the past, to establish with irresistible force the strength of our position? What do we need save a simple exposition of our struggles to make our claims such as the most bigoted or hostile must perforce acknowledge them!

It is time to return to the question of equality of prestige, which forms part of the Catholic claim. I have said that it requires that the new College should be co-ordinate with Trinity College, under a common University, and that the students of the two Colleges should have to pass a common Examination as the qualification for the University degree. This will give to the degree that will be conferred on Catholics a value at least equal to that of the Trinity degree at present. But it will not give them with equal facility an equal share in the prestige that the name of Trinity carries with it. Ireland, and even Catholic Ireland, is justly proud of Trinity College, and of its many distinguished scholars and mathematicians. The fact that it is an essentially Protestant institution should not blind us to its claims on our admiration, and, I would almost add, our love. The Catholics of Ireland, strong in the strength of their Holy Faith, can afford to be tolerant as none else can afford it. They are tolerant, more tolerant than the most liberal among Protestants, tolerant with the true toleration that is founded on the conscious possession of Truth. Every educated Catholic in Ireland will bear me out in the assertion that if Catholics were to be free to deal with other religious bodies in Ireland as they please, they would deal with them one and all with not only justice, but generosity. Episcopalians, Wesleyans, Presbyterians, even the Orangemen of the North, would have no reason to complain of the treatment they would receive from their Catholic fellow-countrymen. And Trinity, above all—Trinity, around which group so many historic memories—Trinity, which has kept alive the traditions of scholarship when the bigotry of the dominant party extinguished so far as it could the light of knowledge throughout the land—Trinity, which has always numbered among its foremost men those who were also names to be remembered in the records of their grateful country—Trinity, which still has scholars and mathematicians in no way inferior to those of the English Universities—Trinity would always, will always, be treated with the greatest respect, nay, reverence, by the whole body of Catholics in Ireland. They do not wish to destroy the prestige of Trinity—God forbid. They rather desire to increase it. What they do desire to destroy is the exclusiveness of its prestige. Trinity is not really benefited but injured by its monopoly. It would profit from a friendly rival. Catholics at present have no share in its prestige, except in the case of the few good Catholics who have passed through Trinity with distinction. But they have a right to share in it, and they believe that by sharing it they will add to it. They will not add to it at first, but as years go on the College which they claim side by side with Trinity, will be the friendly rival of the Protestant College, and by the impulse that its presence will give to the older institution, will raise the standard within its walls.

For we must remember that Trinity by no means absorbs the main part of the talent of even the young Protestants of the country. Recent statistics prove this very clearly. A comparison has been made between the previous performances of the sixteen boys who every year gain entrance Exhibitions at Trinity and the thirty who gain similar Exhibitions at the Matriculation Examinations of the Royal University. They have been traced through the various grades of the Intermediate Examinations. The results thus gained bring out two curious and significant facts. The one is that the Exhibitioners at the Royal University find it necessary in order to attain a good place to leave an interval of a full year after passing the Intermediate Examination, whereas the Exhibitioners at Trinity in a large number of cases gain their scholarship with a much shorter interval. The other is the still more significant fact that the Trinity Exhibitioners are not as a rule to be found in such high places in the

Intermediate Examinations as the Exhibitioners of the Royal University. I do not forget that the Exhibitioners of the Royal University include among their numbers Protestants as well as Catholics, and up to the present time a considerable majority of them have been Protestants. But the Catholic Exhibitioners are sufficiently numerous to give a clear indication that when the best men of the future Catholic College shall contest with the best men of Trinity College for the mastery in a common University, the former will not be found wanting, and will gradually take their full share in the present honours, and so indirectly in the past prestige of the Protestant College which hitherto in practice has been the sole resident University for Catholic Ireland.

I need not linger long on the third sort of equality of which we have spoken. Equality of local position, of convenient buildings, of suitable lecture-rooms, of facilities for teaching—all go hand in hand with equality of endowment. We cannot expect them all at once to be provided for us with any final sufficiency. Rome was not built in a day, and a Catholic College cannot be constructed and furnished in a week. The elaborate system of rewards and prizes which stimulates Protestant students can only be gradually incorporated, so far as it is desirable that it should be incorporated, in a Catholic College. We cannot look for a generation of mathematicians all at once who shall be skilled in the latest developments of the higher branches of science, but we shall gradually attain to it. We cannot hope for a territorial demesne to spring into existence for our benefit, equal in extent to and situated as favourably as the lordly park which occupies the very heart of Dublin city. But practically no serious difficulty will present itself in regard to this or any other of the material requisites, which can be secured by a sufficient grant of money. The Catholic claim will be met in a liberal spirit as regards buildings, lecture-rooms, recreation-grounds. If all that is needed is not provided immediately, it will not be from any want of generosity, but because some of the appliances necessary to the full equipment of a University College are of more permanent value if gradually supplied, than if they are forced into existence before the time has come when they can be employed to the best advantage.

But I have no intention of descending to details. My task has been to explain, as far as we can, what is meant by the equality which Catholics claim in the matter of Education. At the present moment, when those in authority have not spoken, it would be presumptuous to put forward any constructive scheme for the future.

To sum up the argument that I have urged, Catholics have a right to equality with Protestants in matters of University Education. To expect an equality proportionate to the population at the present time would be most unreasonable. An absolute equality would be really no equality at all. But we can claim, and we do claim, an equality of endowment for Catholics, proportionate to the number of Catholic boys as compared with Protestant who are ready to avail themselves of University Education. These are, roughly speaking, 14 to 11 of the whole body of students, and 14 to 8 of that higher class who obtain some sort of honours and distinctions. Hence Catholics can claim, as a matter of equality and justice, a yearly sum of money which shall bear to the sum allotted to Protestants the proportion of at least 14 to 11.

Besides equality of endowment, Catholics have a right to equality, as far as may be, of prestige. This can only be granted them by the establishment of a Catholic College side by side with Trinity, and enjoying all the same privileges under a common University, comprising all the talent of the nation, whether Catholic, Episcopalian, or Presbyterian.

Lastly, Catholics can claim equality of situation of buildings, of grounds, of educational appliances. All this cannot perhaps be given at first, but it should be recognized as their right from the very beginning and gradually conceded to them as it may practically be found convenient. Thus and thus only can they have a settlement of their claims which can be regarded as in any sense final, and which will satisfy their just demands.

APPENDIX.

ON THE DISTINCTION BETWEEN A UNIVERSITY AND A COLLEGE.

I HAVE more than once stated in the preceding pages that in the plan of University Education that I advocate for Ireland, I do not contemplate the establishment of a Catholic University, but of one or more Catholic Colleges which are to be united with other Colleges under a common University. It may perhaps be well to draw out a little more at length the distinction between a University on the one hand, and a College on the other, as the difference between them is not always very clearly understood. Unless it is present to the mind of the reader, the plan that I am proposing loses all its significance, and a hundred very legitimate objections at once suggest themselves.

There are two important distinctions which mark off a University from a College. The first of these belongs rather to the Universities of the past, when the range of human knowledge was more restricted than it is now, than to any now existing University, at least in these northern lands. In mediæval times a University was a learned corporation, the object of which was to train the intellect in the various branches of study which were then included in a liberal education. These comprised Grammar, Rhetoric, and Philosophy, which went by the name of the *Trivium*, and the four mathematical sciences of Arithmetic, Music, Geometry, and

Astronomy, which made up the *Quadrivium*. Theology, be it noted, was no part of the general University course. A College, on the other hand, attempted no such universality, but was content to give instruction in some special science or branch of learning. Nay, it sometimes would be simply a corporate body of students, gathered together under one roof for the purpose of studying at the University, the College itself not undertaking, as such, any part of their intellectual training. It simply sheltered and controlled them while they were attending lectures in the University. This was the beginning of the present Colleges of Oxford and Cambridge; and it was only gradually that they developed the present system of teaching which exists within their walls.

The modern idea of a University is a somewhat different one. The growth of knowledge has rendered it impossible that a University should include all the branches of knowledge which might claim to be comprised under a liberal education. The advance of the empirical sciences above all has led to a continually increasing specialization of study, and anything like universal knowledge has become more and more unattainable. This led to a gradual change in the idea of a University. Its distinguishing mark was no longer the generality of its training, or the inclusion in the prescribed course of the chief of the liberal arts and sciences. What characterizes the modern University is rather the power to confer degrees in various subjects, which are indeed a testimony on its part that he who receives them has had something more than a mere technical training, but yet do not carry with them the same notion of general culture which had prevailed before. Other external influences produced another change in the connotation of the word University. In order to encourage self-cultivation and self-improvement, residence was dispensed with by some Universities as the condition of the degree, which consequently only meant that the recipient possessed a certain amount of book knowledge, and not that his mind had been formed, and his character moulded by three or four years spent under able teachers, and in contact with men of his own age, who were pressing forward to the same goal that he had in view. No sort of training was necessary beyond the training of the self-trained. Private study was sufficient for achievement of a University degree, and non-resident Universities bid for members by ignoring one of the most important benefits attaching to University life. My task is not to estimate the advantages and disadvantages of the change. I bring it forward merely because it accentuates the contrast between a University and a College. A University confers degrees and does not necessarily imply residence. A College does not confer degrees and does imply residence.

The modern College includes every sort of teaching institution for old or young. There are Colleges for the study of classics, and Colleges for the study of mathematics, and Colleges for the study of engineering. There are Colleges of medicine, and Colleges of surgeons, agricultural Colleges, and Colleges of shorthand, and Colleges for imparting almost every sort of instruction of which the human mind is capable. College has also in some cases retained its old Latin meaning of a Corporation, as in the College of Heralds. I dismiss all these except the one sort of College which concerns us at present, and which, by reason of a sort of approximation to a University, had given occasion to the prevailing misconception.

A University College has this special characteristic, that it is necessarily a College in connection with a University. More than this, it implies that it teaches, if not all, yet the most important branches in which the University with which it is connected examines: and it prepares students for the University degrees. It, moreover, implies residence, either within its walls or in such close proximity as may enable its students to attend its lectures. A University in the modern sense need have no students at all, as in the case of the London University. But a University College implies lectures at which students attend, and which shall be preparatory for University degrees.

We may illustrate this by University College, London, which is a true University College in connection with the London University; by the University Colleges of St. Stephen's Green and Blackrock, in connection with the Royal University of Ireland, and by the Colleges of Oxford and Cambridge. These last, however, are rather Colleges of the University than University Colleges, inasmuch as their teaching is supplemented by the teaching of the University Professors, and there are some subjects which no College as such professes to teach at all. Trinity College, Dublin, is also essentially a University College. It is not a University, but it is a College, at present the only College, under the University of Dublin. The University is a separate corporate body conferring degrees and not requiring residence. Trinity College, on the other hand, as a College, cannot confer degrees, and does require residence.[1] As is often the case, the general ideas of mankind respecting

[1] It is true that it presents a small proportion of students for University degrees who have not resided at all, but it does this merely on account of its being the only College under the University of Dublin, and the bridge over which all must pass who desire a Dublin University degree.

the nature of Trinity are confused and misty, although the name of College, given it by common consent, declares its true character. It is but one College under what was intended to be a National University.

Of late years another University has grown up, and already is the rival both in numbers and talent of the University of Dublin. This is the Royal University, which is described by its Chancellor as the focus of the intellectual life of the country. We need not discuss whether of the two Universities shall become the National University under which the various Colleges shall be grouped. But a National University is the ultimate goal of Irish Education, and until this is attained, no true friend of Ireland will rest content.

The present scheme then proposes to add to what exists already a Catholic College, and (if it so please the Presbyterians) a Presbyterian College also. As Keble College was added to the existing colleges of Oxford to their advantage and to the advantage of the University itself, so the addition of a Catholic College will injure none, and will benefit all. It will injure no one, for it will leave untouched all the privileges of Trinity College, prestige, lands, buildings, endowments, revenues, &c. It is not, as some newspaper writers imagine, to be a College *in* Trinity, as if Catholics desire to thrust themselves into her walls or to occupy a part of her grand domain. It need not even be in the immediate neighbourhood of Trinity, for the matter of that, since a National University need not be a local University, but may justly remain content with the functions of an examining and learned body, which shall keep up the standard of science and scholarship among the subordinate Colleges. Nay, it need not even be a single College, but the central institution in the metropolis might gather around itself other well equipped Colleges elsewhere, closely joined to it in a moral, but not a local, unity.

Such a College will benefit all by the healthy competition it will introduce. When a young horse (to quote the apt illustration employed by one of the speakers at the Catholic Club where the second of my two papers was read), has a rival cantering by his side, his paces are sure to be far better than when he has to run alone, unstirred by the wholesome fear of being beaten in the race. So in the common curriculum of a National University, Catholic and Protestant will improve their own paces, as well as those of their rivals, by the friendly struggle for fame and name and honours.

www.ingramcontent.com/pod-product-compliance
Lightning Source LLC
Chambersburg PA
CBHW020227090426
42735CB00010B/1613